KINDLING
the Heart

*Nurturing Young
Christ-like Servant Leaders*

SUSAN STEEGE

KINDLING *the Heart*

Copyright © 2020 KINDLE
Published by KINDLE
Minneapolis, Minnesota

Book cover and interior design by Gregory Rohm

Printed in the United States of America

– TABLE OF –
Contents

— A WORD ABOUT KINDLE —

MICHELLE PAVASARS

The mission of the Karpenko Institute for Nurturing and Developing Leadership Excellence (KINDLE) continues to be:

To foster and multiply Christ-like servant leaders to enhance the ministries of congregations in their communities and the world.

KINDLE's role in "fostering and multiplying Christ-like servant leaders" focuses on equipping second chair ministry leaders to grow professionally and personally as Christ-like servant leaders. At the same time, they create ministry environments that encourage Christ-like servant leader development of those they serve.

KINDLE truly believes that we are all called to a Christ-like servant leader identity that is lived out in our congregations, homes, workplaces, and communities. Jesus gives us guidance in Matthew 20 and Mark 10 regarding the way that He expects His followers to behave. His way is to serve. While it sounds so simple and obvious, daily experience suggests that being a Christ-like servant leader in today's world demands intentionality and discipline.

We designed this book to encourage parents, grandparents and other Christ-like servant leaders as they commit to raising up children with a Christ-like servant leader identity. Our prayer is that you will be blessed as you focus on nurturing the Christ-like servant leader identity of the younger members of the Church. We also pray that these young Christ-like servant leaders will impact their families, friends, teammates and neighbors as they seek to be the hands, feet and heart of Jesus to those they meet.

We invite you to learn more about KINDLE training and resources at KINDLEservantleaders.org. Follow us on Facebook or Instagram for additional encouragement as a Christ-like servant leader. If you would like to support KINDLE's ministry, consider a donation through our website or gift additional copies of this devotional to your friends and family. Additional copies can be purchased through Amazon.

— FOREWORD —

DR. WILLIAM O. KARPENKO, III

Through a series of meetings during 2000-01, the KINDLE Program Team of Steve Arnold, Jack Giles, Alan Gunderman, Bill Karpenko, and Sue Steege, much like a family of Christian brothers and sisters, created the following servant leader definition:

A KINDLE Servant Leader helps others celebrate their baptismal identity, become more Christ-like, and commit to the development of others as Christ-like servant leaders.

While this definition has been strengthened by adding Christ-like to servant leader, three questions are still regularly posed during KINDLE training experiences:

Are those being served daily celebrating their baptismal identity as children of God?

Are those being served growing more Christ-like, manifesting the grace-filled marks of obedience, well-being, leadership, and community?

Are those being served committing to foster and multiply generations of Christ-like servant leaders in their homes, workplaces, congregations, communities and the world?

Accompanying this definition and set of questions are the Strands, Practices, and Grace-Filled Marks of the Christ-like servant leader. See pages 114-117 for the complete list.

Undergirding these devotions is this wonderful encouragement for you and your family from Philippians 2:5-7 (NIV):

"In your relationships with one another, have the same mindset as Christ Jesus: Who, being in very nature God, did not consider equality with God something to be used to his own advantage; rather, he made himself nothing by taking the very nature of a servant."

May you and your family continue to grow into the fullness of Jesus Christ through this devotional, ever looking for ways to be God's Christ-like servant leader in your unique family, school, workplace, congregation, and neighborhood.

— TIPS FOR FAMILIES —

AUDREY DUENSING-WERNER

In our baptism when the Word is spoken and the water poured, we receive a watermark that shapes who we are and whose we are. It is our identity. We are sealed by the Holy Spirit and marked with the cross of Christ forever.

To be a Christ-like servant leader in our homes is to grow and live out that baptismal identity, knowing that we are united with Christ and that He lives through us to love and serve others.

How can we continue to grow our families into Christ-like servant leaders?

Establish family rhythms, rituals or liturgies using *"Kindling the Heart".* These family liturgies are familiar patterns that permeate everyday life together as a family. They are repeated to help children connect to Christ and to each other in a meaningful way.

Here are simple liturgies that can be a part of family time as you use the "Kindling the Heart of Families" devotional.

CONNECT:

An important part of growing as a Christ-like servant family is to carve out a moment when your household can pause and be fully present with God and one another. This could be in the morning at the breakfast table. Or it could be in the car heading to or coming home from school.

Before you open the devotional, take a moment and CONNECT. A fun way to do that is by using the words JOYS, JUNK, and JESUS. Share one joy from your day. Share a junky part of your day. Share how you saw Jesus in your day.

SCRIPTURE AND SONG:

As you begin, light a candle or a crack a glow stick or even find a battery-operated candle to turn on each night as a reminder that Christ is the Light of the World. A candle or glow stick often times creates a sense of a quiet space or sacred space. Open up God's Word and the "Kindling the Heart of Families" devotional. At the end of the devotional sing a favorite hymn or play a favorite God song.

PRAYER AND BLESSING:

Praying for each other is so rich. Pray for the person beside you. Pray about things that were shared during the connect time or pray about something that was shared during the devotion time.

You may want to find a special bowl that becomes your blessing bowl and fill it with water each night. Dip your finger in the bowl and make the sign of the cross on the forehead, looking them in the eye and sharing their name. Create a family blessing to say together. Maybe it's a part of a scripture verse or maybe it's as simple as "(Name), you are a baptized and beloved child of God."

CELEBRATE:

Before you blow out your candle, celebrate together. Celebrate birthdays and baptismal birthdays but also celebrate ways that God has used you today to love and serve others as a Christ-like servants.

PARTS OF EACH DEVOTION:

In each devotion you will find

BIG IDEA   TALK ABOUT THIS   PRAYER   TRY THIS

Baptized and Beloved Child of God

Scripture:

But now, O Jacob, listen to the Lord who created you. O Israel, the one who formed you says, "Do not be afraid, for I have ransomed you. I have called you by name; you are mine."

ISAIAH 43:1

BIG IDEA:

You are a baptized and beloved child of God!

Have you ever seen a passport? A passport is an official document that you need to show when you travel, especially when you travel to another country. It has your picture in it and your name and your birthday, and it tells the security people exactly who you are and where you live. If you have been baptized, your baptism names you as His child. When you were baptized, God took ahold of you and He will never let go. He did this because of His great big love for you. If you are ever feeling like you don't know who you are, remind yourself that you are a baptized and beloved child of God. It is who you are because God says so!

TALK ABOUT THIS:

How could remembering that your family members are baptized
and beloved children of God change the way you talk to them?

What are some other things God says about who we are?

PRAYER:

Heavenly Father, thank You for loving me so much.
Help me remember that I am Your baptized and
beloved child every day. Amen.

TRY THIS:

***Turn to the person on your right, use
their name and say, "(Name), you are a
baptized and beloved child of God."***

Roots and Fruits

Scripture:

But the Holy Spirit produces this kind of fruit in our lives: love, joy, peace, patience, kindness, goodness, faithfulness, gentleness, and self-control. There is no law against these things!

GALATIANS 5:22-23

BIG IDEA:

Everything starts with God!

What do you know about the roots of trees? Roots grow down into the ground and they do two things for trees. They soak up water and pull it up into the tree. Trees need water to live and to grow. The roots also grow "out" under the ground, and they give the tree support and keep it stable. The leaves and fruit that grow on a tree start underground with the roots. It's the same with us! We want to learn to be servant leaders, to lead like Jesus—and it all starts with our relationship to Him. Our roots are found in worship, in talking with God, and in reading His Word. Every good fruit in us has its roots in God!

TALK ABOUT THIS:

What could we do that would help us
get to worship more often?

Where do you see one of the fruits of the Spirit
(in the Bible passage above) in our family?

PRAYER:

Heavenly Father, I want to dig my roots deep into You.
As I worship You and talk with You and read Your
Word, take hold of my heart and help me live with love.
Amen.

TRY THIS:

*Google "tree root system images" on
someone's phone and look at the pictures
or draw a picture of a tree and talk
about the different parts.*

Name Some Names

Scripture:

One Sabbath day as Jesus was teaching in a synagogue, he saw a woman who had been crippled by an evil spirit. She had been bent double for eighteen years and was unable to stand up straight. When Jesus saw her, he called her over and said, "Dear woman, you are healed of your sickness!" Then he touched her, and instantly she could stand straight. How she praised God!

LUKE 13:10-13

BIG IDEA:

God wants you to notice the people around you!

Have you ever seen someone walking along and looking at their phone? There are people all around them, but when their head is down, they are missing them all. Jesus was exactly the opposite—He was always noticing people. He paid attention to the people around Him and what they needed, like the woman who was stuck bent over in the Bible passage above. A great way to go through any day is to notice the people God has in your life and what God is doing in their life. He wants you to join in!

TALK ABOUT THIS:

Come up with as many names as you
can of people that you saw yesterday.

Share one thing you noticed about someone
God brought into your life yesterday.

PRAYER:

Jesus, I want to notice people the way You did when
You were here on earth. By Your Holy Spirit, help me
pay attention to the people You bring into my day.
Amen.

TRY THIS:

*Choose one person in your life outside
your family (at school, in your
neighborhood, at work, etc...) and
pray for them every day this week.*

Wherever you go...

Scripture:

Live wisely among those who are not believers, and make the
most of every opportunity. Let your conversation be gracious and
attractive so that you will have the right response for everyone.

COLOSSIANS 4:5-6

BIG IDEA:

Your family is a launching pad.

Whenever a rocket ship launches, there is a launching pad underneath
it. A rocket is not meant to stay on the pad—it's meant to go into
space to collect important information that helps people on earth.
It's the same with you—you aren't meant to stay in your house with
your family forever. God made your family a great launching pad so
He could send you into the world and join Him in His work there.
There are people at your school and in your neighborhood and at
your workplace who don't know the love of Jesus. Your family is put
together by God to love each other and grow together in God's
love so that you can share His love in all the places you go.

TALK ABOUT THIS:

Who is someone you know that needs to experience God's love in Jesus? Draw a picture or make a card to give to that person.

What does it mean to "let your conversation be gracious and attractive to others"?

PRAYER:

Jesus, I know You are already at work in all the places I live, work, and play. Show me what You are doing and help me join in. Amen.

TRY THIS:

Choose one person in your life outside your family (at school, in your neighborhood, at work, etc...) and pray for them every day this week.

— PRACTICE 1 —

Embrace Sabbath Living

BIG IDEA:

It's God's plan for us to work and to rest.

Rhythm is an important part of music. It is the beat. Try clapping twice, then pause and clap once. That's rhythm. God's Word tell us that our lives are to have a rhythm, too. He knows that we like to go-go-go. So, He gives us the gift of a commandment that says, "Go-go-go for six days, but on the seventh day, REST." This means that our school work, chores, and other work are holy, and so is REST. Even God rested at the end of creation! One of the ways God shows His love to you is to ask you to regularly rest and worship Him. Sometime, imagine yourself curling up in God's lap and taking a rest. Ahhhhhh.

TALK ABOUT THIS:

What is your favorite way to rest?

What could our family do to slow down and rest together?

PRAYER:

Dear God, we want to live in the rhythm that
You gave us. We need You to help us work hard
and rest well. In Jesus' name, Amen.

TRY THIS:

Rest one day this week.

– PRACTICE 2 –
Learn and Live Scripture

Scripture:

People do not live by bread alone, but by every word that comes from the mouth of God.

MATTHEW 4:4

BIG IDEA:

The Bible feeds your soul.

When you are hungry, really hungry, you can feel it in your body. Your stomach grows and grumbles. Your head feels light and wobbly. And food tastes so good when you're hungry, doesn't it? There is another place in you that gets hungry—the place in your heart where you connect with Jesus (called the soul). Jesus wanted us to know that God gives us food to feed our bodies, and He also gives us His words to feed our souls.

Here's what this looks like: we read God's words often and think about His words and do what His words say. And our souls get filled up with God and His love. Yum!

TALK ABOUT THIS:

Is there a particular verse from the Bible that our
family could take and hold on to this week?

Is there someone you know who might be hungry for
God's Word? How could we share it with them?

PRAYER:

Jesus, Your words fill up my heart and give me life.
Thank You. Amen.

TRY THIS:

***Write a verse from the Bible on your
bathroom mirror with a dry erase marker.***

— PRACTICE 3 —
Pray Uneceasingly

Scripture:

Now you are my friends, since I have told
you everything the Father told me.

JOHN 15:15

BIG IDEA:

Prayer is talking with your friend, Jesus.

Think about the friends you have. What do you like to talk with them about? What happened at school? Something that makes you laugh or scares you? What you had for dinner and why you liked it? Good friends talk about lots of different things. Talking with friends makes life more fun and interesting. One amazing thing that Jesus said is that you are His friend. Wow! The Son of God calls you His friend. You can talk to Him about anything and everything, too. That's what prayer is—talking with your friend, Jesus. You can talk to Him about big things and little things. He's always there and he's always listening. He is the best friend, ever!

TALK ABOUT THIS:

What are some thoughts or feelings you have had
lately? Can you talk with Jesus about them?

What does it mean that Jesus calls you His friend?

PRAYER:

Jesus, it is amazing that You call me Your friend.
I love you. Amen.

TRY THIS:

Tell Jesus about your day.

– PRACTICE 4 –

Witness Willingly

Scripture:

I will not die; instead I will live to
tell what the Lord has done.

PSALM 118:17

BIG IDEA:

Telling others about God starts with noticing what he's doing.

Can you see the wind? No you can't, but you know it's there. You can see what the wind does: rustling leaves on the trees or filling up the sail on a boat. Can you see God? No you can't, but you know He's there. You can see what God does: creating a beautiful sunset, or caring for you when you're sick, or giving you yummy food to eat, or a friend to talk to when you're lonely. When you get really good at noticing what God is doing, it won't be long before you'll be able to tell someone how awesome He is.

TALK ABOUT THIS:

What do you notice about God?

What do you see in God's creation that
tells you something about Him?

PRAYER:

Heavenly Father, You are awesome. I see Your work all
around me every day. Give me some chances
to tell someone else what I see. Amen.

TRY THIS:

Notice five things that God did today.

— PRACTICE 5 —
Serve Others

Scripture:

For even the Son of Man came not to be served but to serve others and to give his life as a ransom for many.

MARK 10:45

BIG IDEA:

God's love gives you what you need to serve others.

Here's the way helping other people works: when you are loved by God (and you are!), you are able to serve other people. God created you and Jesus died for you and now the Holy Spirit will use you to help people who are poor or sad or scared. Do you know someone who needs a friend or a hug or some food? Knowing you are loved by God, be that friend, give that hug, or share some food. Think of Jesus throwing His arms open for you and then throw your arms open for someone else. You were made to do it!

TALK ABOUT THIS:

Is there someone who could use our family's help?

How can we serve the people who live around us?

PRAYER:

Dear Jesus, thank You for serving me and giving Your life for me.
Help me to love the people around me in Your name. Amen.

TRY THIS:

***Brainstorm some ways you could
help people in your neighborhood
and plan the first step.***

– GRACE-FILLED MARK –
Obedience

> ## *Scripture:*
> Remain in me, and I will remain in you. For a branch
> cannot produce fruit if it is severed from the vine, and you
> cannot be fruitful unless you remain in me.
>
> JOHN 15:4

BIG IDEA:

Living the way God wants us to live is a great way to live!

We know that God cares about the things we do and say and He gives us lots of help to know how we should live—in the Bible. Even better than that, He promises to give us His strength and the Holy Spirit's power to live that way. So if you have trouble being kind, or you hurt a friend, or you lie about something, that's the time to go to Jesus and ask for help.

The more connected we are to Jesus the more easily we live His way. It's like fruit that naturally grows from a tree. Our good choices come naturally when we're connected to Jesus and His love.

TALK ABOUT THIS:

How does prayer keep you connected to Jesus?
Reading His Word?

What else helps you be aware of Jesus?

PRAYER:

Jesus, it's so good to know that You love me and live in me.
Help me live like someone who is loved. Amen.

TRY THIS:

Put an empty chair for Jesus in your circle.

– PRACTICE 1 –

Recognize God's Call

Scripture:

For we are God's masterpiece. He has created us anew in Christ Jesus,
so we can do the good things he planned for us long ago.

EPHESIANS 2:10

BIG IDEA:

Finding out how God shaped you is your job for the rest of your life.

There is no one like you! God made you completely unique from
anyone else on this planet. No one else thinks like you do, or
loves others the way you do, or prays the way you do. That's cool,
but it gets even cooler: God made you the way you are because
there are things on this earth that need to be done with Him that
only you can do. So start paying attention to how God made you.
Here are a couple questions you can start with: What ways of
helping others are the most fun for you? What are you good at?

TALK ABOUT THIS:

Share with each family member some way that
God has created them special.

What is unique about our family?

PRAYER:

Heavenly Father, thank You for a creating me in a
special way. Be with me as I learn more and more what
that special way is. Help me listen for Your voice to
tell me who I am. In Jesus' Name, Amen.

TRY THIS:

*Post a piece of paper for each member of the family
in a prominent place in the house that everyone
can access. Throughout the week, notice and write
down a positive thought or characteristic about
individual family members.*

— PRACTICE 2 —

Pursue Wellness

Scripture:

Thank you for making me so wonderfully complex!
Your workmanship is marvelous—how well I know it.

PSALM 139:14

BIG IDEA:

God gave you your body and helps you take care of it.

Your body is amazing! God knew exactly what He was doing when He put together your bones and blood vessels and heart and eyes. And then He gave you that body to take care of so that He can use it for good things. When you eat healthy food (hello carrots!) and move your body (run and jump!) and get good sleep (snuggle in!), it's like saying "thank you" to God for the body He gave you.

TALK ABOUT THIS:

What are three healthy foods you really love to eat?

What are some ways we could move more together as a family?

PRAYER:

God, thank You for making me! Help me make choices that take good care of the awesome body You gave me. Amen.

TRY THIS:

Try a new way to move.

– PRACTICE 3 –
Grow in Wisdom

Scripture:

Don't copy the behavior and customs of this world, but let God transform you into a new person by changing the way you think. Then you will learn to know God's will for you, which is good and pleasing and perfect.

ROMANS 12:2

BIG IDEA:

God made your brain and He wants you to use it!

Your brain is just simply amazing! Did you know that the blood vessels in your brain are almost 100,000 miles long? The brain weighs about three pounds (about the same weight as a toaster). Information runs between things called neurons in your brain for everything you see, think, or do—sometimes as fast as 250 miles per hour! Wow, God is an awesome Maker. He gave you your brain so that you can think and learn and grow. It's important to practice thinking and learning because God may want to use your thoughts or ideas to help someone else. Plus, it's fun to learn new things about God's world!

TALK ABOUT THIS:

What topic would you like to learn about?

How might God want you to change the way you think?

PRAYER:

Heavenly Father, You are the Maker of all things. I love learning about the world You made and using my brain to find ideas. Lead me by Your Holy Spirit to thoughts and ideas that will help me and others. Amen.

TRY THIS:

Learn the meaning of a word you don't know.

– PRACTICE 4 –

Optimize Finances

$Scripture$:

The earth is the LORD's, and everything in it.

PSALM 24:1

BIG IDEA:

Everything you have, including your money, belongs to God!

Think about this: if your friend gave you her bike to use, wouldn't you be extra careful with it? Wouldn't you treat her bike the way she would want you to treat it? Since everything in the world belongs to God, we understand that the things we have are His, given to us to use. This includes our money. When we understand that our money is God's money, we use it the way He talks about in the Bible. We give money, we save money, and we spend it on things that help others. It's an amazing way to live!

TALK ABOUT THIS:

Is there something you would like to
save your money for? What is it?

Which is easiest for you: giving money, saving money,
or spending money? Why?

PRAYER:

Heavenly Father, thank You for the money You have
provided for our family. Keep us open to how You
would want us to give, save, and spend it. Amen.

TRY THIS:

***Put some money together as a family
and spend it to help someone.***

– PRACTICE 5 –
Stay Connected

Scripture:

Dear friends, let us continue to love one another, for love comes from God. Anyone who loves is a child of God and knows God. But anyone who does not love does not know God, for God is love.

1 JOHN 4:7-8

BIG IDEA:

God made you to have friends and be a friend.

Because God made you and He is love, you are made to love others and be loved by others. It's like God's love gets poured into your heart until it overflows and gives you what you need to be kind to and connected to other people. God, of course, has made you His friend, but He also wants you to have earthly friends and be a friend. Taking time to talk with and play with and share with your friends is just how God wants you to live.

TALK ABOUT THIS:

Who, specifically, can you be a friend to this week?
What will you do?

Name some things you are grateful for
about a friend or friends.

PRAYER:

Jesus, I am amazed that You call me your friend.
Help me to be a good friend to others. Amen.

TRY THIS:

***Face-time with a friend or relative you
haven't connected with in a while.***

— GRACE-FILLED MARK —

Well-being

BIG IDEA:

Healthy habits are gifts from God!

Think of a beautiful tree—standing tall, stretching its branches and leaves to the sky. Trees that are planted by water grow especially well because their roots reach out and take in exactly what they need (water) every day. It's the same for our bodies and minds. When we give our bodies, minds, and relationships what they need by making healthy choices, we also stand tall, reaching our hearts to God. As we learn healthy habits, we understand that they are not punishments but gifts from God that He uses to make us whole and well. He gives us what we need!

TALK ABOUT THIS:

What is one healthy habit that you enjoy?
What is one that is hard for you?

How can we encourage each other to make healthier choices?

PRAYER:

Heavenly Father, thank You for creating me and for
giving me the gift of healthy habits. Please help me
make healthy choices more often. Amen.

TRY THIS:

***Pick one healthy habit to
work on as a family.***

– PRACTICE 1 –

Set the Example

Scripture:

Don't let anyone think less of you because you are young. Be an example to all believers in what you say, in the way you live, in your love, your faith, and your purity.

1 TIMOTHY 4:12

BIG IDEA:

Being a good example is one thing you can do to help others make good choices.

Have you noticed that you can "catch" people's attitude, just like you can "catch" their cold? When one brother is crabby, another brother or sister is more likely to be crabby. When one friend makes a good choice, another friend is more likely to make a good choice. God asks us to lead by example. And the best way to do that is to keep our eyes on Jesus. The Holy Spirit connects us to Him and that's how we can act and choose what's best.

TALK ABOUT THIS:

Are there friends with whom I find it
easier to make good choices?

How can we help each other lead by example?

PRAYER:

Heavenly Father, I thank You for the gift of Your Son
Jesus, the best example. Help me keep my eyes on Him
and be His kind of example to others. Amen.

TRY THIS:

*Watch for a chance this week to have
a good attitude when the people
around you are crabby.*

— PRACTICE 2 —
Voice the Vision

Scripture:

But you are not like that, for you are a chosen people. You are royal priests, a holy nation, God's very own possession.

1 PETER 2:9

BIG IDEA:

A family is a great place to remind each other who God says you are.

It's funny how easy it is to forget who you are—who God says you are. We sometimes feel like we don't belong anywhere, but God says, "I chose you." We sometimes wonder if what we do matters, but God says, "you are royal priests." We sometimes think that no one cares about us, but God says, "You belong to me." When we forget who God says we are, our family can remind us—and in fact, saying these things out loud to each other really helps.

TALK ABOUT THIS:

How can we help each other remember
that we are chosen by God?

What are some other things we need
to remind each other?

PRAYER:

Heavenly Father, You tell us we are chosen by You and
belong to You. Give us chances to tell others who You say
they are and help us use Your words to do it. Amen.

TRY THIS:

***Turn to a family member and say:
"You belong to God!"***

— PRACTICE 3 —
Equip to Multiply

Scripture:

You have heard me teach things that have been confirmed by many reliable witnesses. Now teach these truths to other trustworthy people who will be able to pass them on to others.

2 TIMOTHY 2:1-2

BIG IDEA:

Jesus followers help each other grow and learn!

There is always more to learn: about God, about God's Word, and about God's world. Learning to do new things is fun. Here's a good way to teach someone how to do something new. Let's use making an ice cream cone as an example:

1. I make the ice cream cone, you watch, we talk about it.
2. You help me make the ice cream cone, we talk about it.
3. I help you make the ice cream cone, we talk about it.
4. You make the ice cream cone, I watch, we talk about it.

When we follow Jesus, we help each other grow and learn— it's how God created us to live.

TALK ABOUT THIS:

What can grown-ups help kids learn?

What can kids help grown-ups learn?

PRAYER:

Jesus, thank You for giving each of us
opportunities to learn *and* to teach. Amen.

TRY THIS:

Kids: teach your parent how to do something.

— PRACTICE 4 —
Spur One Another

Scripture:

Instead, commission Joshua and encourage and strengthen him,
for he will lead the people across the Jordan. He will give them
all the land you now see before you as their possession.

DEUTERONOMY 3:28

BIG IDEA:

Sometimes God is asking you to help someone else lead the way.

Sometimes leaders lead. Sometimes they help others lead. The
Bible tells us about a man named Moses who was a great leader.
God used him to lead His people out of slavery and through the
wilderness. They were headed to the land God had promised
to His people. At the end of Moses' life, God had a new job for
him: to help Joshua lead the people into the Promised Land.
God asked Moses to encourage and strengthen Joshua for this
new challenge. Sometimes God is asking you to lead. Sometimes
God is asking you to help someone else lead by challenging
them to be or do what God has in mind. He will help you do it.

TALK ABOUT THIS:

Is there anything about the way God made someone in your family that you think they don't realize about themselves?

Share the names of people in your school or neighborhood or workplace that you think you could help. How could you be helpful?

PRAYER:

Heavenly Father, send Your Holy Spirit to help us see how we might help the people around us as they work, play and lead. Amen.

TRY THIS:

Tell someone what you notice about how God uses them for His good.

— PRACTICE 5 —

Encourage One Another

BIG IDEA:

Use your words to help the people around you!

Think about the wind. You can't see the wind, but you can see what it does when the leaves move and the curtains blow. Words are the same way—you can't see them, but you can see what they do when people are hurt or helped. That's because words have the power to hurt or to help. When you use your words to encourage someone else, those words help that person become more of who God made them to be. It's easy to encourage someone—it starts with noticing what's special about what they do or who they are and telling them about it.

TALK ABOUT THIS:

Name some words or phrases that help and
encourage (for example, "Good job!").

How does it feel when someone uses their
words to encourage you? How does it help?

PRAYER:

Heavenly Father, I am tempted to use my words to
hurt others sometimes. I am sorry. Help me use my
words to encourage the people around me. Amen.

TRY THIS:

***Use your words to encourage
someone this week.***

– GRACE-FILLED MARK –

Leadership

Scripture:

But Jesus called them together and said, "You know that the rulers in this world lord it over their people, and officials flaunt their authority over those under them. But among you it will be different. Whoever wants to be a leader among you must be your servant, and whoever wants to be first among you must become your slave. For even the Son of Man came not to be served but to serve others and to give his life as a ransom for many"

MATTHEW 20:25-28

BIG IDEA:

The best leaders lead by helping people.

Jesus was trying to help his friends understand that for people who follow Jesus, leading looks different than it might look in the world. Jesus knew that most people lead by bossing people around and talking about how important the leader is. Jesus said, "Among you it will be different." And then He told them that if they want to lead, they do it by serving, not by bossing around. And He not only talked about it, He also led by example. He told them that even He (the Son of God!) came not to be served, but to serve others and even give away His own life so that others can live. Wow!

TALK ABOUT THIS:

How can we get better at noticing
what the people around us need?

Is there anyone at school or at work or in our
neighborhood that we could serve? How?

PRAYER:

Jesus, You are King of all and Servant of all.
Help me to follow Your lead and understand
greatness as serving others. Amen.

TRY THIS:

**As a family think of five ways that Jesus
served others. (Hint: Open up to one of
the Gospels if you need an assist!)**

– PRACTICE 1 –

Build the Community

Scripture:

Let the message about Christ, in all its richness, fill your lives. Teach and counsel each other with all the wisdom he gives. Sing psalms and hymns and spiritual songs to God with thankful hearts.

COLOSSIANS 3:16

BIG IDEA:

We follow Jesus together!

When God puts a family together, He knows what He is doing. Our family is created by God to walk together in our friendship with Jesus. That means we practice what God's Word teaches us about how to live. We tell each other the truth, even when it's hard. When hurt happens, we practice forgiving each other. We talk about what we're thankful for. We pray for each other and with each other. We aren't a perfect family, but God is building us into the family He has in mind.

TALK ABOUT THIS:

How can we keep Jesus at the center of our family?

What is one thing you are thankful for today?

PRAYER:

Jesus, I am thankful You put me in this family.
As we follow you, help us to practice what Your
Word says about how we live together. Amen.

TRY THIS:

Pray for another family you know.

— PRACTICE 2 —

Identify Common Vision

Scripture:

Holy Father, you have given me your name, now protect them by the power of your name so that they will be united just as we are.

JOHN 17:11

BIG IDEA:

God can use your family for His good!

Look around. Look at the places you live and work and play. Who are your friends? Are there people near you who are scared or sad or sick? Look at your family. What do you enjoy doing together? What are you good at? Singing? Playing ball? Cooking? Hugging? Now ask God to show you where your gifts connect with people nearby who might need your family's help. God shows up to help your family work together for His good—so great!

TALK ABOUT THIS:

What are some things we like to do together?
Some things this family is good at?

Who are some friends who are scared or sad or sick?
How can we help them?

PRAYER:

Jesus, thank You for putting our family
together in a way that is special. Show us
who we can help this week. Amen.

TRY THIS:

***As a family, choose someone
to help this week.***

– PRACTICE 3 –
Promote Communication

Scripture:

Don't use foul or abusive language. Let everything
you say be good and helpful, so that your words will
be an encouragement to those who hear them.

EPHESIANS 4:29

BIG IDEA:

You help everyone in the group when you communicate.

We are all part of different groups. Think of a family,
a classroom, a workplace, or a friend group. Whatever
group you are in, it is important to keep learning how to
communicate—to say how you are feeling and what you are
thinking with words that encourage others rather than tear
them down. How do you know if you are using the right
words? The Bible says make them "good and helpful."

TALK ABOUT THIS:

Name as many groups as you can
think of that you are a part of.

What is one thing you can do to build up
communication in one of those groups?

PRAYER:

Jesus, I know that words matter. By Your Holy
Spirit, help me use words that are good and
helpful to the groups I am a part of. Amen.

TRY THIS:

Say something kind to someone today.

— PRACTICE 4 —

Manage Anxiety and Conflict

Scripture:

When I refused to confess my sin, my body wasted away, and I groaned all day long.

PSALM 32:3

BIG IDEA:

Your family is a great place to practice forgiveness!

When God made Adam and Eve, He made them perfect and they got along all the time. When they sinned, the world was broken and that means people don't always get along. It seems like it's especially easy to get annoyed with the people we love the most: our family. That's not fun. The good news is that Jesus came to forgive our sins, which means a family is a great place to practice owning up to what we do wrong. Keeping it bottled up inside isn't good for you. And a family is also a great place to practice forgiveness. We forgive each other because Jesus forgave us.

TALK ABOUT THIS:

What makes it hard to admit when
you've done something wrong?

Is there someone you have a hard time forgiving?

PRAYER:

Heavenly Father, thank You for sending Your
Son Jesus to make things right and forgive my
sins. Help me to forgive others, too. Amen.

TRY THIS:

***Offer forgiveness to
someone this week.***

– PRACTICE 5 –
Nurture Collaboration

Scripture:

He makes the whole body fit together perfectly. As each part does its own special work, it helps the other parts grow, so that the whole body is healthy and growing and full of love.

EPHESIANS 4:16

BIG IDEA:

Your family is a great place to work together!

Have you ever seen a rowing crew in a race? Eight people (a "crew") sit in a skinny boat called a "shell", one right behind the other. In order to win the race, they have to row exactly together. At the end of a race, they talk about the most important thing: how they worked together. It is the same for groups and families: God made us each different, but He wants us to work together. If you sometimes find yourself fighting against someone in your family, stop and with God's help, see what you can do to work together.

TALK ABOUT THIS:

Name a time when your family has worked
together well. What was that like?

Share one of the special gifts
each person brings to your family.

PRAYER:

Jesus, help each one of us to do our own special
work in our family so that by Your grace our
family is healthy and growing and full of love.
Amen.

TRY THIS:

**Find something your family
can work on together.**

– GRACE-FILLED MARK –
Community

Scripture:

Live in harmony with each other. Don't be too proud to enjoy the company of ordinary people. And don't think you know it all! Never pay back evil with more evil. Do things in such a way that everyone can see you are honorable.

ROMANS 12:16-17

BIG IDEA:

Purposefully doing things that help your family grow is God's idea!

Here's a big word: "cultivate". Cultivate is an action word that means purposely doing things that help something grow. It's used a lot of times when talking about plants or other things that grow in the ground. It works for families, too! When you and your family members purposefully do things that are good for your relationships, you are cultivating your family. Learning how to speak the truth in love, forgiving each other and working together (all things God helps us do), are ways to purposefully do things that result in a loving family who's following Jesus.

TALK ABOUT THIS:

How have you seen our family grow in the last year?

How can we offer the gift of forgiveness to
someone in our family this week?

PRAYER:

Jesus, we thank You for this family. Help us to love
each other well and do things that help our family
grow closer to You and closer to each other. Amen.

TRY THIS:

***Set aside some time this week
to play games as a family.***

– PRACTICE 1 –

Embrace Sabbath Living

Scripture:

He lets me rest in green meadows; he leads me beside peaceful streams. He renews my strength.

PSALM 23:2-3

BIG IDEA:

God wants to restore you when you are tired.

Have you ever been around a puppy? It is so fun to watch them run, wrestle, and play. They go-go-go and then, all of a sudden, right in the middle of everything, BOOM, they lay right down and sleep. Their body just says, "Now it's time to rest—lay down and do it." God is like that for us. He wants us to rest, too. And He wants us to have the kind of rest that really puts us back together. That happens when we rest in Him—by reading His Word and talking to Him and praising Him. Do you hear God saying, "It's time to rest in Me"?

TALK ABOUT THIS:

Why is it hard to stop and rest in God?

How can we make time to walk God together as a family?

PRAYER:

Dear God, we like to go-go-go. Help us to also stop regularly and get some rest in You. Amen.

TRY THIS:

Find five minutes to be silent as a family and listen for God.

— PRACTICE 2 —

Learn and Live Scripture

Scripture:

It is the same with my word. I send it out, and it always produces fruit. It will accomplish all I want it to, and it will prosper everywhere I send it.

ISAIAH 55:11

BIG IDEA:

When you read the Bible, it's not just you working on the Bible, the Bible is also working on you.

God's Word, the Bible, is different than any other book. A man named Martin Luther said this about the Bible: "The Bible is alive, it speaks to me; it has feet, it runs after me; it has hands it lays hold of me." He meant that God's words, when we read them and think about them actually help shape what and who we love and how we think. The Bible is a gift from God that can work in our hearts and minds to help us be aware of God's love for us and help us follow Jesus and live like He did.

TALK ABOUT THIS:

How does reading God's Word help
when you are anxious or sad?

What is one thing you've learned about
God from reading or listening to the Bible?

PRAYER:

Heavenly Father, Thank You for the gift of the
Bible. Make us excited to connect with it every
day. Use it to shape us for Your good work. Amen.

TRY THIS:

*Each day this week, read or listen to
Hebrews 4:12. Memorize it as a family.*

– PRACTICE 3 –

Pray Unceasingly

Scripture:

Don't worry about anything; instead, pray about everything. Tell God what you need, and thank him for all he has done. Then you will experience God's peace, which exceeds anything we can understand. His peace will guard your hearts and minds as you live in Christ Jesus.

PHILIPPIANS 4:6-7

BIG IDEA:

One of the best things you can do when you are worried is talk to God.

God knows you, inside and out. He knows what makes you so happy you want to shout, and He knows what makes you sad or scared. He is not surprised when you worry about things and He wants to help you. The Bible tells us exactly what to do when we are worried about something: "Tell God what you need, and thank him for all He has done." Prayer is a gift God gave us because He wants us to talk with Him. The same God who made everything wants you to tell Him what you need. Is that because He doesn't know what you need? No—He knows what you need. He just longs for you to talk with Him. What an amazing God!

TALK ABOUT THIS:

What are some things you've been worrying about lately?

What can we thank God for that we have seen Him do?

PRAYER:

Heavenly Father, I am so thankful that
You want me to tell You about my worries.
Thank You for loving me so much. Amen.

TRY THIS:

***Practice telling God about your
worries when you have them.***

— PRACTICE 4 —

Witness Willingly

Scripture:

The man who had been freed from the demons begged to go with him. But Jesus sent him home, saying, "No, go back to your family, and tell them everything God has done for you." So he went all through the town proclaiming the great things Jesus had done for him.

LUKE 8:38-39

BIG IDEA:

You can share how God has helped you in your life.

God is so big. He does thousands (no millions!) of amazing things. It might seem like He is so big and so amazing that you are not smart enough or big enough to tell others about Him. But that's just it: all you are asked to do is get to know God better and better and then be ready to tell others what He has done for you. Has He helped you be brave when you were scared? You could tell about that. Has He given You His love for each day? You could tell about that. You don't have to tell the whole story of God, just your story of God. Ask the Holy Spirit to help you!

TALK ABOUT THIS:

What is one way God has helped you?

Where is one place you see God at work around you?

PRAYER:

Heavenly Father, I am so thankful to get to know You better each day. Help me to be ready to share with someone else what I know about You. Amen.

TRY THIS:

***Practice using your words
to tell who God is to you.***

— PRACTICE 5 —

Serve Others

Scripture:

God has given each of you a gift from his great variety of spiritual gifts. Use them well to serve one another.

1 PETER 4:10

BIG IDEA:

You are part of God's plan to make things right in the world.

Ever since Adam and Eve sinned the first time and everything in the world was broken, God set about to make things right. The biggest way He did that was sending His Son, Jesus, to die for all of our sin. He also has in mind to use each of us to be part of His plan to help the hurting, share His love and forgiveness, feed hungry people, or give clothes to people who need them. We sometimes forget to look around us for people who need help, but when we do, God uses us to be His grace in a hurting world. How great is that?

TALK ABOUT THIS:

Is there anyone nearby who is hurting or in need
that God might be calling our family to help?

Is there a broken relationship that God
might be calling you to mend?

PRAYER:

Dear Jesus, thank You for Your amazing work in the world.
Help me notice what You're doing and join in. Amen.

TRY THIS:

***Think together about what a
friend or neighbor might need.***

– GRACE-FILLED MARK –

Obedience

Scripture:

Dear friends, you always followed my instructions when I was with you. And now that I am away, it is even more important. Work hard to show the results of your salvation, obeying God with deep reverence and fear. For God is working in you, giving you the desire and the power to do what pleases him.

PHILIPPIANS 2:12-13

BIG IDEA:

God is working in you so you will want to do what
He says and you will be able to do it, too!

When children are very little, they are often heard saying, "Watch this, Daddy!" or "See what I can do, Mommy!" Knowing they are loved by their parents, they want to do things their parents will like. It is the same with you and God. Knowing God loves you, you want to do the things He wants you to do. And it's even cooler than that because God is also working in you through His Holy Spirit to make you want to do the things God wants you to do. AND He is giving you the power to do them. We don't obey God because we're afraid of Him. We obey Him because He loved us first and we want to show Him our love, too.

TALK ABOUT THIS:

How can we remind each other that God is working in us?

What makes it hard to feel God's power in us?

PRAYER:

Heavenly Father, I am so glad I can come close to you in prayer. By Your grace, give me what I need to take actions that grow our relationship. Amen.

TRY THIS:

Find a worship song on YouTube (search for the song and "lyrics") and sing it together.

– PRACTICE 1 –

Recognize God's Call

Scripture:

For he is our God. We are the people he watches over, the flock under his care. If only you would listen to his voice today!

PSALM 95:7-8

BIG IDEA:

You can learn to listen for God's voice.

Imagine you are in a room full of people talking and your eyes are closed. As you listen carefully, would you be able to pick out your mom or dad or brother or sister's voice? You sure would. It's the same with God's "voice". There will be many people who want to tell you who you are and what you can do. The most important person telling you who you are and what you can do is God. How will you know it's Him? He will let you know through His Word and when you are talking with Him. He has a call on your life. That means He has created you specially and has work for you to do. Start listening!

TALK ABOUT THIS:

What makes it hard to know
what God wants you to do?

Is there something God is calling
you to do today? What is it?

PRAYER:

Heavenly Father, there are so many voices around
me telling me who I am. Help me learn to listen for
Your voice and take action on what You are calling
me to do and who You are calling me to be. Amen.

TRY THIS:

*Have everyone talk at once. See if
you can make out what a particular
person is saying in the noise.*

— PRACTICE 2 —

Pursue Wellness

Scripture:

Jesus grew in wisdom and in stature and in favor with God and all the people.

LUKE 2:52

BIG IDEA:

Learn to feed the body God gave you with healthy food.

God was on His "A-Game" when He made you. He gave you your mind, heart, and body and wants you to use all of them as you follow Jesus every day. That means that what you eat and drink matters. The body that God gave you works best when you eat healthy foods like protein and fruits and vegetables. Watch for foods that have beautiful colors like strawberries and green beans and kiwi—they are usually good for your body. If you try a healthy food and don't like it, don't stop trying it. Sometimes you learn to like the things that are good for you.

TALK ABOUT THIS:

Is there a healthy food we could agree to try as a family?

What is something healthy we can cook together?

PRAYER:

God, You have given me such good and healthy
food to eat. Thank You! Help me to choose
foods that help my body work best. Amen.

TRY THIS:

***Try something new
and healthy to eat.***

— PRACTICE 3 —
Grow in Wisdom

Scripture:

> God gave Solomon very great wisdom and
> understanding, and knowledge as vast as the sands of
> the seashore. In fact, his wisdom exceeded that of all
> the wise men of the East and the wise men of Egypt.
>
> 1 KINGS 4:29-30

BIG IDEA:

God loves to answer prayers for wisdom!

In the Bible, a king named Solomon had the chance to ask God for anything. Did He ask for more money? No. Did He ask for a long life? No. Did He ask God to kill his enemies? No. He asked God to give him wisdom. Wisdom is knowing the right thing to do—what God would say is right. Solomon wanted to be a good king who ruled well, and so he asked God for wisdom. The Bible says that God was really happy that Solomon asked for wisdom—and He gave it to him! He gave him "very great wisdom and understanding and knowledge as vast as the sands of the seashore. Wow! God will give you wisdom, too, if you ask for it. It's a prayer He loves to answer!

TALK ABOUT THIS:

Who do you know that is wise?
Why do you say that?

Where do you need God's wisdom today?

PRAYER:

Heavenly Father, I want to be wise and helpful.
I am bold to ask You for Your wisdom so that
I can be useful to myself and others. Amen.

TRY THIS:

Ask God for wisdom.

– PRACTICE 4 –

Optimize Finances

BIG IDEA:

Money, like a lot of things, grows best little by little.

Jesus followers understand their money is not their money—it belongs to God. And since your money is God's money, you learn what He says about money in His Word, the Bible, and you take actions on what He says. The Bible has a lot to say about money! One thing it says is that it is smart to save money little by little, over time. Many things grow a little bit at a time (including people). When you save money, even a little money, bit by bit by bit, it grows. You will be amazed to find out how it works!

TALK ABOUT THIS:

What makes it hard to save money?

Is there anything about money that
we could talk about together?

PRAYER:

Heavenly Father, we know that everything we have
comes from You and belongs to You, including our
money. Help us learn more and more how to save
money and use it as You would want us to. Amen.

TRY THIS:

***Save one dollar a week and
see what happens!***

– PRACTICE 5 –
Stay Connected

Scripture:

We are confident that as you share in our sufferings,
you will also share in the comfort God gives us.

2 CORINTHIANS 1:7

BIG IDEA:

God gave you the people in your life
for good times and bad times

Connections with family and friends are one of God's
best gifts! He knows that when we are connected to other
people there are times when we can share fun and laughter.
It's God's idea that we have fun and laugh together—it's
good for us! It's also God's idea that we are connected
during sad and scary times. He uses us to comfort each
other and love each other and pray for each other. That's
good for us, too! We have lots of chances to remind each
other that we're not alone and that God is with us.

TALK ABOUT THIS:

Is there someone (or someones) our family
could share some fun with?

Is there something we could do to make
the connections in our family stronger?

PRAYER:

Jesus, thank You for the connections with
friends and family that You have given me. Help
me share comfort and joy with them. Amen.

TRY THIS:

***Write a note to someone
who is sad or sick.***

– GRACE-FILLED MARK –
Well-being

Scripture:

Even youths will become weak and tired, and young men will
fall in exhaustion. But those who trust in the LORD will find
new strength. They will soar high on wings like eagles. They
will run and not grow weary. They will walk and not faint.

ISAIAH 40:30-31

BIG IDEA:

God wants us to be well and whole.

It is awesome when you feel good and strong and well and whole.
Times like this are times to say, "Thank You God!" and ask how
He might use your good and strong and well and whole self to help
someone else. What about when you don't feel that way? What
if you are sick or sad or scared? We all have times like that. Guess
what? Times like that are also times to say, "Thank You God" for
the things you do have and the people who love you. And they are
also good times to ask for God's help. The Bible says that when we
trust in the Lord we "find new strength." So whether you are
feeling great or not so great, turn your heart to Him.

TALK ABOUT THIS:

Name the doctors and other health professionals
in your family's life and say a prayer for them.

What helps you when you're feeling sick? Tired? Sad?

PRAYER:

Heavenly Father, no matter how I'm feeling, I am
thankful for the many ways You take care of me.
Please continue making me well and whole. Amen.

TRY THIS:

***As a family, reach out to someone
who is sick with a text or a card.***

– PRACTICE 1 –
Set the Example

Scripture:

And you should imitate me, just as I imitate Christ.

1 CORINTHIANS 11:1

BIG IDEA:

Noticing how Jesus acted and acting like
Him is the best example for others!

People who follow Jesus can learn so much about how to live and lead by watching how He acted and spoke. There is so much to learn from Jesus that it could take up a thousand books, but here are a few things He did: Jesus noticed people who were hurt or sick or poor or sad and spent time with them. Jesus loved people that most people hated. Jesus spoke kindly to people who had a loved one who died. Jesus spoke up when people were being treated unfairly. What would happen if we lived by Jesus' example? We can't do it on our own, but the Holy Spirit will help us be an example to others by following Jesus' example.

TALK ABOUT THIS:

What do you love about Jesus?

What makes it hard to live like Jesus?

PRAYER:

Heavenly Father, I thank You for the gift of Your Son
Jesus, the best example. As I follow Him, give me
Your Holy Spirit's power to lead by example. Amen.

TRY THIS:

***Spend time with
someone who is lonely.***

– PRACTICE 2 –

Voice the Vision

Scripture:

"For I know the plans I have for you" says the LORD.
"'They are plans for good and not for disaster,
to give you a future and a hope.'"

JEREMIAH 29:11

BIG IDEA:

When life is wild and crazy, remind
each other that God is for you!

Life in a family can get wild and crazy. Everyone is busy,
busy, busy. There is work and homework and housework
and sports. People are sometimes crabby or annoyed or
mad or sad. There are birthdays, school, work, and doctor's
visits. Sometimes when life gets wild and crazy, we forget
that God has a plan. And it's a good one, full of hope.
So when life gets wild and crazy, one thing you can do
is remind each other that God has a good plan for your
family, one meant to give you a hope and a future.

TALK ABOUT THIS:

What do you think God's good plan
for our family includes?

What are some things we could pray
for about our family's future?

PRAYER:

Heavenly Father, it is so good to know that You have a
plan for our future and that it is good and full of hope.
We trust You and we love You. Amen.

TRY THIS:

***Write out the words of
Jeremiah 29:11 on the
bathroom mirror with
a dry-erase marker.***

– PRACTICE 3 –

Equip to Multiply

Scripture:

For God is the one who provides seed for the farmer and then bread to eat. In the same way, he will provide and increase your resources and then produce a great harvest of generosity in you.

2 CORINTHIANS 9:10

BIG IDEA:

Being a leader means checking in on how others are doing.

You might think that being a leader is about being "in charge" and bossing people around, but it's not. It's not about getting your way, either. When we follow Jesus' example, we know that being a leader is about serving and helping the people around you. That means we ask ourselves questions about the people around us. "How is my sister doing? How could I help her?" or "Is there an encouraging word or hug that would help my dad?" or "What chore could I do that would help my mom?" or "What special treat would my son enjoy?" Jesus' example of leading is always one that helps and serves others.

TALK ABOUT THIS:

Who do you know that is good at focusing
on others and helping them?

Who around you would you like to
know better in order to help them?

PRAYER:

Jesus, You show me in so many ways that
Your idea of greatness is service. Teach
me to grow more like You. Amen.

TRY THIS:

**_Think of a person you could invite to
spend some time with your family._**

— PRACTICE 4 —

Spur One Another

Scripture:

Let us think of ways to motivate one
another to acts of love and good works.

HEBREWS 10:24

BIG IDEA:

There are times when we need to hear
hard things about our choices.

In this family, we are "for" each other. We want the best for each
other. We see God's good work in each of us. We also know
that each of us (grown-ups and kids alike) are sinners. We make
mistakes. We hurt each other. Because of this, and with God's
help, we want to learn how to speak the hard words to each
other. We want to learn how to hear those words, too. God says
when we speak hard words with love, we're on the right track.
Let's ask God to help us keep learning how to do this well.

TALK ABOUT THIS:

What are some "acts of love and good works"
that we could do as a family?

What helps you stay calm when someone
is sharing hard words with you?

PRAYER:

Heavenly Father, Teach me by Your
Holy Spirit, how to speak hard
words in a loving way. Amen.

TRY THIS:

***Share your love for someone
before sharing hard things.***

— PRACTICE 5 —

Encourage One Another

Scripture:

When the uproar was over, Paul sent for the believers
and encouraged them. Then he said good-bye and
left for Macedonia. While there, he encouraged the
believers in all the towns he passed through.

ACTS 20:1-2

BIG IDEA:

God calls us to encourage the people around us!

Can there ever be too much encouragement? When we lead by
serving others (like Jesus did), we know that what we spend time
thinking about and focusing on, grows. If we spend time thinking
about what we don't like about someone, or about what they are
doing wrong, those "not good" things will get bigger in our hearts
and minds. On the other hand, when we spend time thinking
about what is good about someone and about what they are
doing that is helpful, those "good" things will get bigger in our
hearts and minds. And then we take the step of encouragement:
telling them how we see God's good work in them.

TALK ABOUT THIS:

The Bible passage above says Paul "encouraged the believers in all the towns he passed through." Take some time as a family to name all the places you each pass through in a week. Who could use some encouragement in those places?

How does it feel when someone uses their words to encourage you? How does it help?

PRAYER:

Jesus, thank You for Your example of leading by serving others. Help me to serve the people around me by encouraging them. Amen.

TRY THIS:

Think of someone that you have negative feelings towards. Brainstorm something you like about them and share it next time you see them.

— GRACE-FILLED MARK —
Leadership

Scripture:

"Don't ever be afraid or discouraged," Joshua told his men. 'Be strong and courageous, for the LORD is going to do this to all of your enemies.

JOSHUA 10:25

BIG IDEA:

You can encourage others by reminding them that God is with them.

When God asked Joshua to lead His people into the land God had promised them, He knew there would be some hard times. As Joshua led, he pointed to God as the reason to be strong and courageous. Anyone can encourage others in this way! Do you know someone who is going through a hard time? Can you remind them that they can be strong and courageous because God is fighting for them? Do you know a group or family or team that is working on something that is a big challenge? Can you encourage them by praying for them and telling them that God is with them?

TALK ABOUT THIS:

Why is hope so important for our family?

How does knowing God is with us give us hope?

PRAYER:

Heavenly Father, You are my hope for
everything in this life. Remind me to turn
to You and turn others to You. Amen.

TRY THIS:

***Hold hands and say this together:
"God is with you! Be strong
and courageous!"***

— PRACTICE 1 —

Build the Community

Scripture:

God places the lonely in families; he sets
the prisoners free and gives them joy.

PSALM 68:6

BIG IDEA:

A family is a good place to go through
the ups and downs of life together!

Think of the kinds of things that happen in life! Someone gets
an "A" on a test: hooray! A friend moves away: booo! Mom or
Dad has a great accomplishment at work: hooray! Someone is
struggling to make good choices: booo! And on it goes. Life
is filled with ups and downs and God knows that. He sees our
happy days and our sad ones and He is with us. He also gave us
our families. A family is a great place to celebrate when something
great happens and to be present when the hard times come. God
meant for us to have that kind of love for each other.

TALK ABOUT THIS:

What helps you when you are feeling down?

What's your favorite way to celebrate
when something good happens?

PRAYER:

Heavenly Father, here we are together—help us be
there for each other in happy times and sad times.
Thank You that we are not alone. Amen.

TRY THIS:

***Find a new way to celebrate
with your family.***

— PRACTICE 2 —

Identify Common Vision

Scripture:

But Caleb tried to quiet the people as they stood before Moses. "'Let's go at once to take the land,' he said. 'We can certainly conquer it.'"

NUMBERS 13:30

BIG IDEA:

Knowing who you are as a family helps you know what to do!

In the Bible passage above, Caleb does something important. God's people were about to go into the country that God had promised them, but they got scared. Some people were saying they shouldn't go. Caleb stayed calm and reminded the people that God had given them what they needed to conquer the land. In families it's a good practice to remind each other who God is and that He has given us what we need to love Him and love people. When we face a challenge, let's remember to remind each other of that. God is with us and wants to use us for His good!

TALK ABOUT THIS:

What are some things God might
want to use our family to do?

What is something our family could do
together that shows our love for God?

PRAYER:

Jesus, thank You for giving our family what we
need to be and do what You want us to. Give us
the courage to love You and love others. Amen.

TRY THIS:

***Write "Loving God and loving
people" on a bathroom mirror
with a dry erase marker.***

– PRACTICE 3 –

Promote Communication

Scripture:

In everything we do, we show that we are true ministers of
God. We prove ourselves by our purity, our understanding,
our patience, our kindness, by the Holy Spirit within us,
and by our sincere love. We faithfully preach the truth.
God's power is working in us.

2 CORINTHIANS 6:4A, 6-7

BIG IDEA:

It's important to talk about what we do together AND how we do it.

There is always a lot going on in families. In order to get everything
done and get everyone where they need to be, there has to be
communication. Parents and kids talk about where they are going
and what they are doing. It's also important to talk about *how* things
get done in your family. You can do that by asking some "how"
questions, like these: "How are we going to talk with each other
when we're angry?" "How will we decide what to do when we don't
agree on what to do?" "How can we encourage each other?" Talking
about "how" is one way God is helping us love each other.

TALK ABOUT THIS:

How will we decide what to do when
we don't agree on what to do?

How will we talk with each
other when we're angry?

PRAYER:

Heavenly Father, help us as a family keep learning
what it means to communicate with each other.
Help us do that with patience and love. Amen.

TRY THIS:

**Set aside some time to
talk as a family.**

– PRACTICE 4 –
Manage Anxiety and Conflict

Scripture:

So get rid of all evil behavior. Be done with all deceit, hypocrisy, jealousy, and all unkind speech. Like newborn babies, you must crave pure spiritual milk so that you will grow into a full experience of salvation. Cry out for this nourishment, now that you have had a taste of the Lord's kindness.

1 PETER 2:1-3

BIG IDEA:

When one person is anxious, it affects everyone

Have you ever seen a mobile? A mobile is a piece of hanging art whose parts are balanced to move when they are touched or blown. When you touch one part of a mobile, every part moves. It's a system. God made families into systems, too. When one person in a family feels anxious or grumpy, it impacts everyone. Because of that, when you feel anxious or grumpy, one of the best ways to help your family is to work through it. You can do that by talking to God or loved ones about what is making you anxious or grumpy. You can do that by moving your body with some exercise. You can do that by writing about how you're feeling. When you work through the hard feelings, it helps everyone.

TALK ABOUT THIS:

How does our family usually handle it when one
of us is grumpy? How would we like to handle it?

In what ways have we "had a taste of the Lord's kindness"?
How might that help us be kind to each other?

PRAYER:

Heavenly Father, when I feel anxious or grumpy,
help me remember that you
love me and want to help me. Amen.

TRY THIS:

Google "hanging mobile images"
on someone's phone.

– PRACTICE 5 –

Nurture Collaboration

Scripture:

May God, who gives this patience and encouragement, help you live in complete harmony with each other, as is fitting for followers of Christ Jesus. Then all of you can join together with one voice, giving praise and glory to God, the Father of our Lord Jesus Christ.

ROMANS 15:5-6

BIG IDEA:

Working together adds up!

Sometimes God's "math" is surprising. For example, God says that when a man and woman get married, it's not "one plus one equals two", but "one plus one equals one" because those two people are one marriage—a thing that God says is very special. Another example is what happens when a team or a family works together. What gets done by a group of five people adds up to much more than what would get done if those five people worked alone. Working together adds up to awesome!

TALK ABOUT THIS:

What is the hardest thing about working together?

What do you like about working together?

PRAYER:

Jesus, we need Your help to learn to work together as a family. Thank You for showing us how to do that. Amen.

TRY THIS:

Hold hands in a circle and say, "We're in this together!"

— GRACE-FILLED MARK —

Community

Scripture:

Two people are better off than one, for they can help each other succeed. If one person falls, the other can reach out and help. But someone who falls alone is in real trouble, Likewise, two people lying close together can keep each other warm. But how can one be warm alone? A person standing alone can be attacked and defeated, but two can stand back-to-back and conquer. Three are even better, for a triple-braided cord is not easily broken.

ECCLESIASTES 4:9-12

BIG IDEA:

God made us to face life's troubles together.

Have you ever broken a pencil in half? It's not hard to do, and sometimes it happens by mistake. Imagine for a second putting three pencils together and trying to break them. It is much harder to do! The Bible uses a word picture like that to tell us how we need each other when times are tough. If you are all alone and you fall down, there's no one to help you up. God made us in a way that we need to have healthy relationships with people so that we're not alone when troubles come. When God is at work (and we know He is) AND we stand together, good things happen.

TALK ABOUT THIS:

How can we keep on growing our
relationships in this family?

What troubles can we talk to God about together?

PRAYER:

God, we thank You that You gave us each other.
Help us learn what it means to help each
other up after a fall. Amen.

TRY THIS:

***Put your hands into the center, one
on top of the other, and stay until
you feel each other's warmth.***

– STRAND 1 –

CULTIVATING *Faith*

KINDLE Christ-like servant leaders practice Christ-like disciplines in the context of community and equip other Christ-like servant leaders to do the same.

PRACTICE 1: **EMBRACE SABBATH LIVING**

Eagerly worship, partake in Holy Communion, and nurture additional behaviors which foster spiritual renewal and rest.

PRACTICE 2: **LEARN AND LIVE SCRIPTURE**

Discover and apply the truths of Scripture in all your comings and goings.

PRACTICE 3: **PRAY UNCEASINGLY**

Pray continually – alone and with others – for all people, the church, and the world.

PRACTICE 4: **WITNESS WILLINGLY**

Accept God's call to be a voice and example of His restoring grace and mercy in your communities and in the world.

PRACTICE 5: **SERVE OTHERS**

Go forth as a living sacrifice, being God's ambassador of reconciliation to all people, especially to the least of these.

GRACE-FILLED MARK: **OBEDIENCE**

Cultivating Faith results in the grace-filled mark of obedience.

— STRAND 2 —

CULTIVATING *Health*

KINDLE Christ-like servant leaders pursue health in all aspects of their life, and equip other Christ-like servant leaders to do the same.

PRACTICE 1: **RECOGNIZE GOD'S CALL**

For emotional health, live out the personal calling for which you have been gifted.

PRACTICE 2: **PURSUE WELLNESS**

For physical health, pursue a balanced lifestyle.

PRACTICE 3: **GROW IN WISDOM**

For intellectual health, intentionally and regularly engage in learning opportunities.

PRACTICE 4: **OPTIMIZE FINANCES**

For fiscal health, pursue behaviors which promote optimal use of God-given financial resources.

PRACTICE 5: **STAY CONNECTED**

For social health, seek the mutual conversation and consolation of other Christians.

GRACE-FILLED MARK: **WELL-BEING**

Cultivating Health results in the grace-filled mark of well-being.

— STRAND 1 —

CULTIVATING *Individuals*

KINDLE Christ-like servant leaders invest in developing
and equipping other Christ-like servant leaders

PRACTICE 1: **SET THE EXAMPLE**

Behave in ways consistent with that of a Christ-like servant leader.

PRACTICE 2: **VOICE THE VISION**

*Elevate the importance of developing and
multiplying Christ-like servant leaders.*

PRACTICE 3: **EQUIP TO MULTIPLY**

*Engage in an intentional, ongoing process of Identifying, Inviting,
Apprenticing, Coaching, and Multiplying Christ-like servant leaders.*

PRACTICE 4: **SPUR ONE ANOTHER**

Challenge others to develop as Christ-like servant leaders.

PRACTICE 5: **ENCOURAGE ONE ANOTHER**

*Recognize and celebrate evidence of growth
in Christ-like servant leadership.*

GRACE-FILLED MARK: **LEADERSHIP**

Cultivating Individuals results in the grace-filled mark of leadership.

— STRAND 2 —

CULTIVATING *Groups*

KINDLE Christ-like servant leaders foster Christian communities in their ministry settings and equip other Christ-like servant leaders to do the same.

PRACTICE 1: **BUILD THE COMMUNITY**

Help groups be transformed into Christian communities.

PRACTICE 2: **IDENTIFY COMMON VISION**

Facilitate groups as they discover their common vision and mission.

PRACTICE 3: **PROMOTE COMMUNICATION**

Speak the truth in love through healthy communication patterns.

PRACTICE 4: **MANAGE ANXIETY AND CONFLICT**

Apply biblical means to both maintain healthy relationships and restore broken ones.

PRACTICE 5: **NURTURE COLLABORATION**

Work together to achieve the group's vision and mission.

GRACE-FILLED MARK: **COMMUNITY**

Cultivating Groups results in the grace-filled mark of community.

Words of Appreciaton

- To **Emily Phoenix**, whose editing skills refined the ideas and language in this book; and **Susan Whited** for grammar help and proofing.

- To **Audrey Duensing-Werner** for her excellent "Tips for Families" which I know will be a help to parents who long for faith conversation with their kids and will be helped to craft those habits by Audrey's wisdom.

- To our artist **Gregory Rohm**, who challenged us to think in new and helpful ways about design.

- To **Jason Christ** and **Michelle Pavasars**, who walked through the creation of this book every step of the way. You are both Christ-like servant leaders to the core.

- To my treasured mentor **Bill Karpenko**, the "K' in KINDLE: you have been a steady, beautiful and Christ-centered influence in my life. You have the gift of spurring and the gift of encouraging. I thank God for you.

- To the Associates and Training Teams of the **Classic KINDLE** learning initiative, for the journey that we've been on to discover what it means to be a Christ-like servant leader and help others to do the same. I wouldn't trade it for anything!

- To the families past and present at **First Trinity Lutheran Church** in Tonawanda, New York: it has been my great privilege to have a front-row seat to these beautiful families for 35 years (and counting). It is a true blessing to see how God puts families together and how He uses them to help us all grow in faith and love.

- And finally to my mom and dad, **Paul** and **Neva Steege** who doggedly led devotions with us Steege kids at every supper we shared together. You pointed us to Jesus and I am forever grateful.

Made in the USA
Middletown, DE
16 January 2023

22204976R00066